GERVASE PHINN

Grandchildren

D

First published in 2016 by Country Publications Ltd
The Water Mill, Broughton Hall
Skipton, North Yorkshire BD23 3AG
www.dalesman.co.uk

Text and editorial selection © Gervase Phinn 2016
Additional text © named contributors 2016
Illustrations © Misato Fujisawa 2016

ISBN 978-1-85568-355-6

306· 87L5

Printed in China for Latitude Press Ltd.

Dedication
In memory of Robert Flanagan (1960-2016),
managing director of Country Publications,
ever-supportive and encouraging, and a good friend.

Introduction

Grandchildren — and grandparents, of course, as you can't have one without the other — are a great source of pleasure and humour. The youngsters gladden our hearts with their innocent and comical comments, while the older generation continue to offer endless wit and wisdom. In this book I have put together a collection of my favourite jokes, sayings and observations alongside my own experiences of being a grandfather. My thanks to those who have contributed to this book via the pages of magazines published by Country Publications, and to my own family for providing the first-hand material.

GERVASE PHINN

Gervase with grandson Harry.

L ast year I became a grandfather for the fourth time. Little Charlotte was born and oh, how small and beautiful she looked when I cradled her in my arms for the first time. I have so many things planned for her. We will walk along the beach at Whitby, paddle in the sea, build sandcastles, explore rock pools for crabs, collect shells and bits of smooth, coloured sea glass, eat sticky candy floss and feed the screeching seagulls on the harbour wall.

She will snuggle up with Grandpa for a bedtime story, help Granny make gingerbread men, squeal with delight at the pantomime and do all the other things little ones so love to do. Everything for her will be bright and new and exciting. Of course, my little grandchild will also make the shrewdest observations, as all young children tend to do:

"Grandpa, your face needs ironing", "Oh, I do like the

A grandparent is old on the outside but young on the inside.

smell of old age", "Have you ever thought that when I'm twenty-one you'll probably be dead?" And she will confound me with the most difficult questions that the innocent child frequently asks: "Why are holes empty?" "Why do you have to talk to God with your eyes closed?" "Grandpa, who will fetch the fish and chips when you're dead?" "Why can't we walk and wee at the same time like cows do?" "Grandpa, why are there more idiots on the road when Daddy's driving?"

When lovely Princess Diana visited the North, crowds came to see her. She knew young children well and had a great empathy with them. Seeing among the children thronging to give her flowers a rather sad little boy with hair like a lavatory brush and a small green candle appearing from a crusty nostril, she went straight to him. He was holding a wilting bloom. She singled him out and, bending low, took the flower and ruffled the child's hair affectionately.

If God had intended us to follow recipes, He wouldn't

"And have you had the day off school to see me?" she asked the child, giving him one of her stunning smiles. "No," he replied bluntly, "I've been sent home with nits!"

Young children are nothing if not honest and their honesty is invariably disarming and comical. At a time in the world where everything seems so gloomy and depressing and there's constant conflict and violence, the words of small children lift our spirits, they help us to feel good about ourselves and others and they make us optimistic for the future.

When her six-year-old grandson came by for his lunch she asked him if his farming dad had got a bull out in the meadow. His reply amused her: "No, but he said this morning that there's a big hullabaloo in the farmyard."

have given us grandmothers. — Linda Henley

"Granddad, we've been asked to take something very, very old into school. Will you come in with me tomorrow?"

Our grandson was visiting us for their Christmas holidays and would persist in shouting up the chimney: "Santa Claus, Santa Claus, I want a bicycle for Christmas."

"No need to shout," I told him, "Santa Claus isn't deaf."

"I know," he replied, "but Daddy is."

"Is your granddad very old?" asked the teacher. The little girl thought for a second before replying, "Well, he's not that new."

I explained to my grandson, aged five, who had asked where my dog was, that Rusty was very old and tired and had had a long and happy life and that the vet had 'put him to sleep'.

"When will you be going to the vet then, Grandma?" he asked.

While having lunch, my small grandson asked casually: "Granddad, can I have your watch when you die?"

Grandmas are mums with lots of frosting.

While recovering from a cataract operation I asked my granddaughter to pick up her toys, explaining that I couldn't bend down yet.

"Why? Will your eye fall out, Gran?" she asked.

Six-year-old, presenting a single lily to her teacher: "I can bring you another tomorrow, Miss. Grannie won't mind, she's not being buried till Thursday."

I was reading my grandchild's schoolbook in which she had written:

Grandparents don't have to do anything except be there when we come to see them.

They are so old they shouldn't play hard or run. It is good if they drive us to the shops and give us money.

When they take us for walks, they slow down near things

When a grandfather gets old and begins telling stories,

like pretty leaves and caterpillars.

They show us and talk to us about the colours of the flowers and also why we shouldn't step on cracks.

One day I looked after my two grandsons, ages six and three, while my daughter had her hair done. When she arrived home the six-year-old told her how beautiful she looked. Then he looked back at me and said, "And Gramma, you look almost beautiful."

A week prior to Christmas, I was shopping with my small grandson in a supermarket. As we passed a freezer, I asked him: "Why do you think that freezer is full of frozen turkeys?"
"To make sure they're dead," he replied.

better eat him. — Sydney Smith, Canon of St Paul's, 1800

On Sunday morning when my father took me to visit my grandmother she always had her meal cooking and I got into the habit of asking for a saucer of meat and potato, the taste of which was so different that it has never been equalled.

The Yorkshire pudding, cooked in one large tin, rose so large that it was almost strong enough to climb without assistance from the oven.

Uncle Arthur, her eldest son, drove steam engines. He always made it in his way to stop when passing through the town to visit, sit at the table, have lunch and marvel at his mother's puddings.

"No gravy for me, I like jam on mine," he would say as he prepared to stuff yet another forkful into his already crammed mouth. I watched in admiration and wonderment at this feat of eating.

"Eeh, our Arthur always loved his food. Specially t' Yorkshire puddings. Fancy coming all this way on his train for Yorkshire pudding."

Roger Ellis

When my granddaughter, who had only just started school, came to visit me I asked her what she had learned. She replied: "If I had four apples and you gave me three more, I should have seven."

"Very good," I said, "and if you had four bananas, and I gave you three more, how many would you have then?"

"Oh," said my granddaughter, looking blank, "we haven't done bananas yet!"

A granddaughter asked her rather diminutive grandfather: "Granddad, why are you so small for your age?"

"When you get to be a big boy," I told my small grandson, aged five, "I will take you to Disneyland."

"I don't think I'll ever get to go," said Miles, sadly, "because I expect you won't be alive when I'm a big boy."

Gran says: "He's as much use as a lump of stale bread."

We were stood at the local churchyard watching a neighbour leaving after her wedding when Gran said: "My, isn't she like her mother. There's neither of 'em needs a mirror."

"What did the doctor say you had then?" asked Grannie when Gramps got back from the surgery.

"Neuralgia," said Gramps.

"Ahh, I thought it were summat new that I hadn't come across afore."

"Grannie," said Bethany, aged five, "I know the 'F' word."

"Oh dear," I said in mock horror, "you must never use that word!"

"I don't, Grannie," she replied. "I say trump."

I don't know who my grandfather was; I am much more

My grandfather was very rich in stories. He told of a farmer he knew who was also the gravedigger at the church. One day, when the farmer had just completed the difficult task of digging a grave in the rocky ground, a walker approached him and said, "I say, that's not a very deep grave you've dug."

This irritated the weary farmer a little. "No," he replied, "but there's none o' them getten out yet."

Granddad said to me: "Just remember that when someone says your grannie wears the trousers in this house that it's who wears the braces that keeps 'em up!"

A granddaughter was tapping away on her toy typewriter. "I'm writing a story," she announced.

"What's it about?" asked Grandma.

"Oh I don't know, Grandma. I can't read yet."

concerned to know what his grandson will be. — Abraham Lincoln

Granddad's Shed

It was a small green painted shed at the bottom of the
*   garden,*
With a sagging roof of grey tarpaulin which bubbled in
*   the summer sun.*
Inside it was dark and musty.
There was a threadbare carpet, an old easy chair and a
*   workbench*
And a black stove with a chimney that went through the
*   roof and churned out black smoke.*
He called it his getaway, his special place, his retreat.
He made things in his shed:
Little carved figures, bird boxes, stools and shelves,
Sawing and planing and fashioning, dust-coated,
Covering the floor with sweet-smelling shavings.
I would sit and watch.
He said little but sometimes looked up and smiled.
He lived until he was ninety
And died in an old people's home.

One very cold day when my mum was young, my grandma asked a neighbour to take her to school. Apparently, Gran's teeth had frozen in a glass of water and she didn't want to be seen without them!

"Why don't you have a home help any more?" I asked my grandma.

"Well love," she explained, "it used to make me so tired tidying up before she came."

When Gran reached her hundredth birthday, the local paper sent a reporter to visit her. "To what do you attribute your long life?" asked the reporter.

"To the fact that I was born so long ago," she replied .

Becoming a grandmother is wonderful. One moment

I once went with my grandfather, a farmer, to the town's auction mart. We were loading up at close and he said: "Are them piglets in?"

"All secure," I replied.

"Did you collect them tools?"

"Under the seat."

"We've got the bran and the meal?"

"Yes, I think that's the lot."

"Then off we go," said Grandfather, and we headed off along the road towards home. But he seemed uneasy and kept on looking round into the cart.

"Nay, I feel uneasy somehow," he said, "as if we'd forgotten something."

When we arrived home, he jumped down from the cart, and as he began to unload he slapped his thigh and exclaimed: "Well, I'm blessed. I know now what were bothering me. We've left your grandma in town."

---

you're just a mother. The next you are all-wise and prehistoric.

Without having much money, my grandparents wanted to find somewhere cheap to get away at the start of their marriage, and decided for their honeymoon upon the Common Cold Research Unit.

There, they were kept in isolation, only allowed out into the town at night when they would not come into contact with anyone else. They only told their parents where they were when they got there, and they were horrified to find out where they had chosen!

My grandparents were paid for going and had all their meals cooked for them. One of them was given the cold virus, and the other given a placebo. However, as it happened, neither of them caught a cold and they enjoyed their stay so much that they decided to go back again the next year for another holiday!

This thriftiness has always continued, and I remember visiting them a couple of years ago, to find my granddad mending a fifty-pence fly swat with twine saved from a sack, wrapped around a splint made from a broken knitting needle, glued across the break in the handle of the swatter.

I asked him why he bothered to spend all this time and effort fixing it, to which he replied, "It will be just as good as it was before when I'm finished, and it's also partly the fun of mending it!" I think it sums up the wartime generation's incredible ability to see potential in everything, and not to throw away or waste anything that could be of use in the future.

Stephen Flatman

Grandmother was constantly at war with Mother over the bathing of children. Grandmother never saw my mother's viewpoint on this. 'Washing away the natural oils.' 'Giving them their death of cold.' 'Making them vain and proud.' All such comments came at regular intervals when Mother would stoke up the fire and pull out the damper.

Roberta Best

The Inspector Calls

(extract from The Other Side of the Dale *by Gervase Phinn)*

I was feeling confident and pleased with myself when I appeared after morning playtime in the classroom of Mrs Dunn. I gathered the small children around me on the carpet in the Reading Corner and we talked about several large colour photographs of various animals which I had brought with me.

I explained that we were going to write some little descriptive poems about the different creatures, which included a mole, rabbit, squirrel and dormouse. We were to look at each picture in turn and it was my intention to encourage the children to talk about the colours and

---

Being grandparents sufficiently removes us from

shapes. I did not, however, get very far. When I held up the large photograph of the mole, one of the older children, a large round child called Thomas, remarked casually that his granddad killed moles.

"Does he really?" I replied equally casually and attempted to move on. "Now look at his little fat black body. He's an unusual little creature, the mole. Can you see his big flat paws like pink spades and the sharp claws? Can anyone tell me what—"

"They dig and dig wi' them claws, deep underground they go and chuck up reight big mounds of soil," explained Thomas to no one in particular. "Do a lot o' damage to a field, do moles. They're a real pest my granddad says. Some farmers put down poison but me granddad traps 'em and hangs up their bodies on t' fence."

I decided to look at another picture. "Here we have a grey squirrel. I saw a squirrel this morning peeping from between

the responsibilities so that we can be friends. — Allan Frome

the branches of the tree outside. Look at his large black eyes and long bushy tail. Can anyone tell me what—"

"Tree vermin," commented the same boy. "Me granddad shoots them an' all. Ruin trees, they do. Me granddad says squirrels are a damn nuisance. They eat all t' corn put out for t' hens.

"Rats wi' bushy tails, that's what squirrels are. Me granddad goes out in t' morning with his shotgun, shoots 'em and hangs up their bodies on t' fence."

"Just listen a moment, will you, Thomas," I said, catching sight of Mrs Dunn sitting at the back of the room with a self-satisfied smile on her face. She seemed to be quite enjoying my discomfort.

"We can perhaps talk about that later on. Now I want us all to look very carefully at this picture of the rabbit. I saw quite a few rabbits this morning as I—"

"Me granddad kills them an' all," said Thomas. "He pegs

It is as grandmothers that our mothers come

a little string net ovver t' rabbit warren holes and lets one of his jills down."

"Jills?" I asked.

"His ferret. He keeps her half fed to make her keen. If he underfeeds her, she eats t' rabbit and won't come up out of t' hole. If he overfeeds her she won't go down at all. He lets her down t' hole and she chases t' rabbits out into t' net. Then me granddad breaks their necks. He's reight good at that."

"Really?" I said feebly.

Thomas, my grandson, all of eight years old, was looking decidedly sad in class.

"Are you all right?" asked his teacher.

"No," Tom replied. "It's been a horrible week," he told her. "First my granddad died and then my pet hamster escaped. It's been one thing after another."

---

into the fullness of their grace. — Christopher Morley

My five-year-old granddaughter was watching me tidying up the kitchen. I asked her what her new teacher was like.

"She's nice but very untidy and a bit lazy," replied Becky. "Do you know she gets an old lady, I think it's her mummy, to clean the classroom at the end of the day?"

We tried to get Granddad out more, so when there was a charity dance at the village hall we asked him if he wanted to buy a ticket. He replied simply, "I never pays to sweat."

My daughter told my grandson to apologise for forgetting my birthday.

He said: "I'm sorry I forgot your birthday, Grannie. I have no excuse and it will serve me right if you forget mine next Friday."

Gran says: "I can sum it up in two words — ridiculous."

Granddad on being asked how he was feeling:
"Well I'm better than I were, but I'm not as well
as I were afore I were as bad as I am now."

A boy was visiting his grandma who lived far away from his
home and whom he hadn't seen since he was a baby. The
first morning when they sat down to breakfast his grandma
asked the small boy to say grace.

"I don't know what you mean," said the boy.

In an endeavour to explain, the grandma said, "Well,
what does your daddy say before you begin eating?"

The boy replied: "Now, think on lad, go steady wi' t'
butter."

Grandma on being asked how long her neighbour
had been dead: "Well, if he'd lived till next
Wednesday, he'd have been dead three weeks."

If I had known how wonderful it would be to

My grandson is not enthusiastic about history. The other day he returned home in a very disgusted state. "Grandpa," he said, wearily, "were you told about Alfred the Great when you were at school?"

"Yes," I said, "but that was a long time ago. Why do you ask?"

"Well, they're still going on about him."

Grannie Always Listens
My grannie never interrupts
She listens and listens to all I say,
And smiles and nods,
And nods and smiles.
She has all the time in the world.
Dads butt in, mums natter,
But Grannie always listens.

BECKY MARSDEN (AGED 11)

---

have grandchildren, I'd have had them first. — Lois Wyse

I was testing my small granddaughter on her use of capital letters and full stops. "Can you tell me where the full stops go?" I asked.

"Of course I can, Grannie," she replied. "We've done full stops at school."

"Where do they go then?"

"You know, Grannie," she said pertly. "You really ought to know by now. If you were in Miss Barrett's class you'd be on the bottom table."

I asked Gran how she was feeling after a short spell in hospital. She replied: "I'm all right now. I've had one of them blood confusions."

My grandfather disappeared about the time of the assizes, and we

My grandmother always referred to the singer Englebert Humperdink as Engledink Humperdick.

My small grandson got lost in the supermarket last week. He approached a security guard and said, "I've lost my granddad."

The guard asked him what was his name, and he replied, "Gramps."

The guard smiled and asked, "What's he like?"

The little boy hesitated for a moment, and then replied, "Famous Grouse whisky."

I looked after my grandson when his school closed for a day. The English teacher had given him some work to do; one question was to write a sentence containing the word 'comfort'. He wrote: "The landlord's comfort rent."

asked no questions. — Sydney Smith, Canon of St Paul's, 1800

I used to live in Leeds and remember bath night in our terraced home. We had a bath in the living room, under the window. It had a heavy wooden top and was my play area when down. On bath night — usually Saturday — the bath tap was hooked up to the wall and we all bathed in front of the fire.

I was always bathed first, coming out in front of a warm fire with a blanket over the clothes horse keeping out the draughts, bliss. I was then packed off to bed, Granddad (aged ninety) would come next, protesting all the way: "I don't need a bath; I am as clean as anyone."

Needless to say my father took no notice and my grandfather was duly bathed and seated in front of the fire saying, "Ee that's grand."

Years later we bought our house (for £300) and we had the bath put in the back attic; it was cold, cold, cold and bathtime was never the same.

Marian Short

About a sharp-tongued woman, Gran would say: "Talking to her was like having tacks spat at you."

My young grandson often helped me in the garden. He had obviously been listening to me for when his tower of Lego collapsed after he had spent a great deal of time on it, he said: "Bugger!" under his breath and then, catching sight of me, added, "Pardon my French, Granddad."

Grandparents are similar to a piece of string — handy to have around and easily wrapped around the fingers of their grandchildren.

Talking about the new neighbours who had just moved in next door, Grandma said: "They must be pretty well-off, they're having a purgatory made for the garden."

Gran says: "He couldn't pull the winkers off a nightmare."

Soon I will be an old, white-haired lady, into whose lap someone places a baby, saying, "Smile, Grandma!" — I, who myself so recently was photographed on my grandmother's lap. — *Liv Ullmann*

> Granddad, on returning home from his allotments, announced that one of the neighbours had died. Grannie said, "How sad." Granddad replied, "Aye, he'd not lifted his taties yet."

I had a bit of a tummy ache after rushing in from playing and gulping down some of Gran's jam roly-poly. She said to me: "It's your own fault . You shouldn't be eatin' hot puddin' out o' t' oven, cold."

> Gran had me in creases when she said: "Some animals inebriate during winter."

Calling a grandfather a sexagenarian sounds like flattery.

Although I love to sing, I am not a very good singer. In fact, I was asked to leave the choir at school because I put the other singers off. When my small granddaughter came to stay I sat her on my knee and started to sing a lullaby. She clamped her hands over her ears and cried, "Please, Grannie, stop! You're hurting my ears!"

When I was younger I asked Granddad what it was like being married. He said: "It's like being a fly on flypaper: alive but not getting away." I can't remember if Gran was in earshot.

Dalesman Grandfather
Old man, smoky beard,
Sunshine smile and haystack hair,
Hands like roots and corn gold skin,
He doesn't have a single care.
Old man, falcon nosed,
Bent old back and raven's eye,
Thin as a scarecrow in his fields,
He stands and sees the world go by.

DANIEL EVANS (AGED 10)

It's such a grand thing to be a mother of a

Talking about electricity board staff working in a nearby field, Gran said: "They're putting up some of them there electric pythons."

Grannie came to visit us and was staring out of the kitchen window at the washing line where our rather grey-looking bed linen was drying. She turned to my mum and asked: "Have you been using that blackberry soap again, Elsie?"

I asked Granddad if he would be voting for his neighbour in the parish council elections. He said, "Shan't be voting for him, his allotment's a right mess."

My grandmother started walking five miles a day when she was sixty. She's ninety-seven now, and we don't know where the hell she is. — *Ellen DeGeneres*

---

mother — that's why the world calls her grandmother.

Years ago when my boyfriend and I visited Grandma he offered to take her for a short ride on his motorcycle. Grandma, a tiny, rather prudish lady, replied, "Oh no, I'd have to put my arms around you and that would never do."

Granddad, talking about his eighty-year-old brother: "Straight as a gun barrel when he was young. Now he has to have one of them there home helps to mollycoddle him, he's that thin. Looks like a lathe in a rabbit skin."

Grandfather told us that he was going to the chiropodist to have an 'intoeing grownail' removed. Always good for a Spoonerism, he once had an injection with a 'hyperdeemic noodle' and visited France on 'the cross-flannel cherry.'

An hour with your grandchildren can make you feel young again …

The relationship between grandparents and their grandchildren is rather different from that between parents and their children. Grannies and grandpas, in my experience, tend to be more patient, better listeners, less critical and, dare I say it, more indulgent than their own offspring.

It was the weekly ritual for my mother, well into her eighties, to come around for Sunday lunch. From her vantage point in the most comfortable chair in the corner of the sitting room, she would watch as my wife Christine and I attempted to bring up our four children.

One Sunday I had occasion to chastise Matthew, then aged six, for his untidy bedroom. Stabbing the air with a finger, I ordered him: "Up those stairs now, young man, and

anything longer than that, and you start to age quickly. — Gene Perret

tidy your bedroom! Do you follow my drift?" Matthew at first looked suitably contrite but then a small smile appeared on his lips, then a grin to be followed by giggles and finally guffaws. I ballooned with anger. Then I caught sight of my mother in the mirror. She was sitting behind me pulling the most ridiculous faces and wiggling her fingers in front of her nose.

"Mother!" I snapped rather pompously. "I am trying to instill some discipline here. You are not helping matters!"

"Oh, do be quiet," she told me. "You're not talking to teachers now."

"Mother ...!" I began.

"Don't mother me. He's a lovely little boy, is Matthew. He's kind, gentle and well-behaved. You should be telling him that, not hectoring him. Goodness me, there are more important things in life than an untidy room and yours was like a tip when you were a boy."

Father and son were stuck for words.

She continued. "I don't suppose I should tell your daddy

off in front of you, Matthew," she said, "but he's wrong."
Then she gave me a knowing look and one of her smiles,
and added, "And he's my little boy."

Having read this account, you will understand why this
poem by Mark Thomas, aged nine, has a particular
resonance for me.

My Nan
I like my Nan.
She's round and wrinkly and powdery
And smells of flowers and soap.
She's as comfy as a cushion to sit on.
When my Mum shouts at me
I go to my Nan.
She cuddles me and says,
"Never mind love,
Your Mum was like that
When she was a little girl
A real grumpybum!"

My grandparents by W R Mitchell

Granddad, born in the Thomas Hardy Country of Dorset in 1866, spent most of his life in the industrialised village of Bradley, near Skipton. Reared at Piddletrenthide, a village with a stone church and some thatched cottages, he emigrated to Burnley, seeking an alternative to farm work. His new environment was almost wholly man-made, with a pattern of terraced houses and mini-forest of mill chimneys breathing dark smoke into the air.

Granddad eventually settled in Bradley, where I regularly met him in his twilight years. He and Selina, his third wife, lived in a housing block known as t' Barracks. He found employment in Green's mill — until he became dissatisfied with the wages being paid to the operatives. Quoting the officially-agreed figures to the boss, he was sacked on the spot. My dad, who stood up for him, also suffered instant redundancy.

They found millwork in Skipton. Granddad continued to live in Bradley, commuting into town on foot and often returning home late, having attended a trade union meeting in the evening.

In the last quarter of the eighteenth century, Bradley, a village with a strong Quaker influence, became a stronghold of Methodism, with two chapels. The Primitives had a plain, box-like place. Further up the hill was the more elaborate Wesleyan chapel attended by the mill owner and his family. To Granddad, "t' Primitive chapil" was a home from home. He became a local preacher and also superintendent of a large, sometimes restless, Sunday School. All this was despite an impediment in his speech.

Years later, I experienced a social highlight at Bradley, being invited by George Green to take the harvest festival services at the hilltop chapel. Afterwards, at the well-furnished mill owner's house, I had tea in a grand setting, in sharp contrast with my grandparents' modest home.

Granddad was a well-read man. My love of the moors began with a dip into his library, which included works by Thomas Hardy and the Brontë girls. Also he loved works on natural history. Granny lived on into her nineties. She was then small, bent and with a wizened face which, at Sunday teatime, became patterned with purple as beetroot juice worked its way between the ridges.

Sunday was a special day. A purple cloth with tassels was spread over the table, on which reposed the Bible and the latest issue of the Methodist Recorder. People talked in hushed tones. Chapel-going was obligatory. Granny played a quiet part in chapel life, her only major outing being a choir trip to Morecambe. We "nivver 'eard last on it".

On an anniversary weekend at the "Prims", a visiting

minister was put up overnight at my grandparents' modest home. He, like Granddad, was fond of smoking a pipe. A cruel trick was played on them. Each was told that the other could not tolerate smoking. A long, twitchy weekend followed. On the last evening, the minister sneaked out of the house, found a secluded place — and lit his pipe. Looking up at the house, he saw Granddad had done likewise and was leaning out of a bedroom window to allow the smoke to disperse quickly. A happy reunion followed.

I saw Grannie most often during the blackberry season, when I frequented old sandstone quarries that were the source of the juiciest berries. I also explored the moors that formed a Brontë-ish backdrop to the village. My grandparents were interred at the hilltop cemetery — from which there is a splendid view of the Aire Valley and the moors beyond.

First published in Down Your Way *magazine*

In a café with my granddaughter, aged six, we waited outside the toilet for an inordinate amount of time. "Whoever's in there is taking their time," I said impatiently. "I think they must have taken root." A moment later a rather large woman emerged. "We thought you were a plant," chimed up my granddaughter.

George, our eight-year-old grandson, came home from school and told us he had been playing with Mr Thomas's circumciser. We discovered later that he had been referring to Mr Thomas's synthesizer.

The great thing about being grandparents is that (although you love your grandchildren dearly) you can give them back at the end of the day.

Granddad was a hoarder of all sorts of odds and ends. When I asked him why, he'd say: "Well, yer see, when yer hasn't got any yer finds yer has some."

Grandparents are the best babysitters. You feel comfortable leaving your baby with them for long periods, which is why most grandparents flee to Bournemouth.

Elephants and grandchildren never forget. — Andy Rooney

A mother becomes a true grandmother the day she stops noticing the terrible things her children do because she is so enchanted with the wonderful things her grandchildren do. — *Lois Wyse*

Granddad

He is bald my Granddad is,
Got no hair at all.
Lots of crinklies round his eyes
And on his cheeks as well.
He laughs at me and Natalie.
His face goes all funny.
Makes wrinkles on his face
Like lots of lines
On my trousers.

LUKE BANISTER (AGED SIX)

Everyone needs to have access both to grandparents and

Grandma used to say, "If you save something when you've got something, you'll have something when you ain't got nothing."

Mum was often upset when Granddad talked about death, but he did her make her smile when he told her that he wanted to be buried near the entrance to the graveyard. "Why's that?" she asked. "So I can get out afore t' rush," he replied.

"Do you get on with your neighbour?" I asked Grandma. She replied: "Well, I don't want to say anything against the man; in fact, if I knew anything good about him I'd tell it you."

Granddad gave me a piece of gardening advice which has stood me in good stead over the years: "Before starting anything do plenty of perhapsing — it'll save a lot of if-onlying afterwards."

When my daughter was pregnant my eldest granddaughter was promised a new baby brother or sister for her birthday. The six-year-old said: "If it doesn't make you too big, Mummy, I'd like a little pony too!"

When I asked my grandson what he'd done at school, he said, "We've had two new lessons, history and geography. They were smashing, but I don't know which was which."

When the second of my children started work my Granddad called and said: "Well, an' how does ta feel now tha's getten another pullet layin'?"

My grandkids believe I'm the oldest thing in the world. And after

We took Gran to an orchestral concert and afterwards asked what she thought. "It's rather wonderful," she said. "If you shut your eyes it's just like being at home listening to the radio."

Granddad always used to tell me the tale of when he visited the doctor after hurting a hand. He'd say: "Doc, when this hand of mine gets well, will I be able to play the banjo?"

"Certainly," said the doctor.

"Thanks, Doc. You're certainly a wonder. I never could before."

Mum asked Gran how she got on when she met an old school friend for lunch. Gran replied: "We were so busy counting each other's wrinkles we didn't take any notice of what we were saying."

---

two or three hours with them, I believe it, too. — Gene Perret

Little girl to her schoolteacher: "Do you know we've got a brand new baby girl at my house this morning?"

Teacher: "Oh, how lovely, I wish I could have a brand new baby girl at our house."

Little girl: "Well, it's very easy. You could have one. All you have to do is to go home, have a hot bath, put on a clean nightie, go to bed and then send for my grandma!"

On starting school, our granddaughter, Emily, had a lovely teacher called Mrs Little and another one who, she told me, was called Mrs Old Lady. Well, we wracked our brains and wondered if it was Mrs Holliday or something similar. When we visited the school, in Cleator Moor, we discovered it was in fact Mrs O'Leary! We all laughed about it — so funny from a little four year old.

Angela Stringer

Gran phoned me to say there'd been a small fire at her residential home; it was a serious matter but she had me in stitches when she said: " . . . and they had to use a fire distinguisher."

Talking of an elderly neighbour, Granddad said: "Well, she turned ninety last week, and she is in good health. She's still got all her facilities." I think he meant faculties!

Granddad was a sturdy octogenarian who often said: "I eats what I like and drinks what I like, then I go to bed and let them fight it out between 'em."

Child: "Granddad, how many days in a week?"
Granddad: "Six Saturdays and one Sunday."

If nothing is going well, call your grandmother. — Italian Proverb

I asked my 104-year-old gran what she thought was the best thing about being her age. She simply replied, "No peer pressure."

My grandparents' garden had a couple of apple trees. Granddad always said to me that the apples were "so tart they'd put your ears back two inches!" I think he was only trying to put me off pinching them though because Gran's apple pies were always gorgeous.

When my three-year-old granddaughter Jane saw snow falling for the first time, she observed: "Come and look, Gran; it's raining rice pudding!"

My granddaughter stared at me for a while before asking, "Grandma, why don't you and granddad have real names like the rest of us?"

Grandmas never run out of hugs or biscuits.

"Wake up, Granddad, this is my new friend, Michael. He hasn't got a granddad and I've brought him in to show him what one looks like."

Grannie came to visit us shortly after we had our first TV installed. She seemed interested but when I asked her if she would like me to install a set in her cottage her reply was: "Nay, Ah don't want all sorts of folk like you have on there coming into my room, acting foolishly and talking rubbish. Besides, Ah don't want folk Ah've never met before looking out o' that box at all my bits and pieces."

I asked my Granddad if he was getting accustomed to retirement. "Oh aye, straight away," he replied. "It were working I never got used to."

I was having a conversation with Granddad about having to wear a clean shirt every day for work. He had worked as a farm labourer in his youth and was astounded at the thought. "My mother used to make me wear a shirt one week in bed and the next on the farm," he said.

My grandmother is over eighty and still doesn't need

We took Granddad to look at a bungalow on a housing estate for when he retired from his job in the countryside. "It won't do for me," he said, "it'd be like living in a barrel and looking through t' bung hole."

We took my Grandma round a farm and slowed down when we came to a field where some harvesting machinery was being operated. She watched in silence, then sighed in satisfaction, saying: "You know, I've always wanted to see a concubine working."

Child: "Granddad, What do you do all week?"
Granddad: "Monday through Friday, NOTHING ...
Saturday and Sunday, I rest."

glasses. Drinks right out of the bottle. — Henry Youngman

My Welsh grandmother once remarked that the new neighbours were clearly middle-class because they had fruit on the sideboard.

Champion Talker

My Grannie says I am a little chatterbox.
She says I talk ten to the dozen.
Chatter, chatter, chatter.
Natter, natter, natter.
My Grandpa says,
"Never mind, poppet.
You take after your grannie.
Chatter, chatter, chatter.
Natter, natter, natter.
She's the world champion talker."

ELIZABETH WHITEHOUSE (AGED SIX)

The best place to be when you're sad is Grandpa's lap.

My fondest memory of Granddad is also my most embarrassing. I was seven years old and at my grandparents' house after school. Granddad was eating his tea and I was engrossed in a book when he asked me if I would like to feed the budgie.

Looking upon this as quite an honour, I accepted with great delight, though I have to admit that I was more than a little surprised when he handed me the bird's food. Accepting that the great man must know what he was doing, I proceeded to push chips and bread through the bars of the cage.

A couple of minutes later the silence was broken by my nan who, upon entering the room from the kitchen, exclaimed, "What on earth are you doing?"

"Feeding Joey, like Granddad said," I replied.

Looking up, and quickly realising my mistake, he responded, "No, I said do you want a chip buttie, not do you want to feed the budgie!"

Tim Gray, Hull

A niece had a grandfather who had very large ears. One day she said to her mother, "When Grandpa dies will he become an angel?" The mother replied, "I expect so, dear, why do you ask?" "Oh, I thought he'd become an elf," replied the child.

The School Inspector Revisits
(extract from The Other Side of the Dale *by Gervase Phinn)*

"Who taught you to turn pages like that, William?" I asked. "Granddad. He's a gret reader is mi granddad. Can't get enough books. When we goes to t' library, he gets reight cross when he oppens a book and sees all them grubby thumb marks on t' bottom o' pages. He reckons you 'ave to 'ave respect for books. That's how yer turn the pages of a book, tha knaas, from t' top."

"Yes, that's right," I agreed.

"'Old a book in your 'and and you're a pilgrim at t' gates of a new city."

I was stunned into silence. "What was that you said?"

"Hebrew proverb," said the boy, scratching the thick

Never have children, only grandchildren. — Gore Vidal

thatch of black hair. "Learnt it off mi granddad. He's a gret one for proverbs and psalms, is mi granddad. He's a preacher, tha knaas."

"A teacher?"

"Nay, a preacher."

"Really?"

"Methodist. He reads his Bible every neet. He showed me how to turn t' pages wi'out damaging t' book. He reckons that John Wesley learnt to read upside down, tha knaas. 'As thy 'eard o' John Wesley?"

"I have indeed," I told him.

"Amazin' man was John Wesley. He was one o' nineteen children, tha knaas."

"Really? I didn't know that."

"They say he travelled near on a quarter of a million miles on his 'orse bringing t' word of God to folks. Spent a lot o' time in Yorkshire did John Wesley."

Of mothers who often leave their children at home

"Amazing."

"He used to listen to his father reading t' Bible to 'im every neet as a little un and he used to follow t' words which were upside down to 'im, o' course. My granddad reads Bible to me. Not upside down, though. I know all t' stories: Samson, Daniel in t' lions' den, Moses, Noah, Jacob, Joseph. There's some lively stuff in t' Bible."

"And which is your favourite bible story?" I asked.

"Waay, it 'ud 'ave to be David and Goliath."

"Why is that?"

"Well, it's a cracking good tale, i'n't it? Old Goliath comes ovver dale, huffin' and puffin' and shoutin' and screamin' and wavin' his reight big sword abaat like there's no tomorra and tellin' t' Israelites to send out their champion. Out comes little David, wi' nowt but a sling shot in 'is 'and. 'Waaaaay!' rooars old Goliath. 'Tha must be jokin'. Is this t' best thy lot can do? Little squirt like thee! I could tread on

---

thee and squash thee. I could spit on thee and drowan thee. I could breathe on thee and blow thee into t' next week. Send out a proper champion, not a little scrap like thee. I'm not feightin' thee.' Anyroad, David says to 'im, 'I'm thee man', and he reaches into t' beck and pulls out a pebble t' size of a pullet egg and pops it in 'is sling shot and lets fly. By the 'eck, it di'n't 'arf shift and it 'its old Goliath smack between 'is eyes."

"That must have really hurt him," I ventured.

"'Urt him? 'Urt 'im?" the boy cried. "It ruddy well killed 'im!"

We were discussing alterations to the local railway station when Grandfather said: "They've knocked the front end down, now you have to get your tickets from a little chaos round the back."

Nobody can do for little children what grandparents do. Grandparents

Granddad was an avid angler and also fond of embellishing his tales. He told this story to me many times about when he fished on a large estate: a stranger approached him and said: "Now, my man, do you know you are trespassing on private grounds and fishing in private waters?"

Granddad said, pulling out his fishing line and relighting his pipe: "And who are you?"

As he walked slowly away the stranger replied: "I am the Duke of Devonshire. All the waters and land are my private property."

"Oh aye, Duke," said Granddad, "And how did you get all this land and property?"

"I received them from my ancestors," replied the duke.

"And how did they get them?"

"They fought for them."

With a twinkle in his eye, Granddad retorted: "Well, I'll fight you for 'em now then."

---

sort of sprinkle stardust over the lives of little children. — Alex Haley

One evening I was with my grandson Charlie on the bus going into town. A youth got on wearing a loud T-shirt on the front of which was emblazoned: 'Tonight I'm Gunna Score!', written beneath a scantily-clothed woman. Charlie stared for a moment at the youth before saying, "I play football as well." The youth looked confused. "And I'm the best scorer in our school team," he added proudly.

Granddad brought home an enormous potato from the allotment and announced to Mum: "You'll have to cut that into three halves to get it in t' pot."

I'll always remember a sweet thing my grandma once said after a friend's husband had a heart attack: "We should have been made with two hearts — one for work and one for loving."

Posterity is the patriotic name for grandchildren. — Art Linkletter

Grandma looked a bit upset when she returned from the garden centre where she'd been to buy a tree to hide an eyesore in the garden. I asked her what had upset her. She replied, "Well when I told the assistant what I wanted, he looked me up and down and said, 'You look about my age so you'll be wanting a fast-growing one then'."

As a little boy aged ten in 1937, I was sent to live with my grandparents for a while by my family. A memory I shall always treasure. One of the joys was going with Grandma to the first-house pictures on Saturday night. During the interval I was treated to a Hokey Pokey (ice cream). Coming out at the end of the show, grandma gave me a shilling to call at the fish shop and get fish and chips three times and a bottle of vinegar. And I got a penny change! Arriving at Grandma's, we sat down at the table with fish and chips covering a dinner plate and a large pot of tea.

Granddad's supper was put on top of the oven to keep warm. We'd finished when Granddad came tottering home from the pub and putting four bottles on the table, he told Grandma that he'd brought her a bottle of beer. (I remember the bottles with a red triangle on the labels.)

Grandma couldn't drink it on a full stomach, so Granddad decided he would drink it. What he did next was very frightening to me, he picked up a bottle and knocked the top off on the edge of the table and drank it! Unfortunately, he'd picked up the vinegar. His outburst of words was strongly painful. Poor Granddad was in a horrible state with a belly full of beer topped up with a bottle of vinegar!

I helped him across the yard to the toilet, and listened to his loud noises in mixed languages. I remember the sky went all funny colours: I thought he was to blame. Now, older, I know it wasn't his fault; it was the Aurora Borealis.

Grandma and I rallied to help with peggy tubs of water. A quick peggy leg and posser soon had Granddad cleaned up again. The next day he went out in cleaned and pressed trousers, completely lost for words — Grandma had pressed his trousers flat with creases at the sides instead of at the front. I told everybody I had the coolest granddad in the village.

Harry Haller

Child: "Granddad, when is your bedtime?"
Granddad: "Two hours after I fall asleep on the couch."

My six-year-old grandson was staying with me and doing some drawing. He stopped and said: "Can I have the pencil sharpener?"

I gazed at him and said: "What's the magic word?"

He looked most perplexed for a few moments and then his face lit up and he beamed: "Izzy Wizzy, let's get busy."

While walking through the council estate to visit Grandma I was surprised to see a ha-ha and a gazebo within a short distance of each other. On mentioning this to Grandma she said: "You must be mistaken. I've lived here for over seventy years and never seen two such birds."

One of the most powerful handclasps is that of a new

While I was driving my grandchildren home we passed a car with a fully made-up clown inside, obviously on his way to a party. The slightly older of the children pointed and said, "Look — it's a clown!"

The younger one thought for a second before replying: "Don't be silly, that's not a REAL clown, that's just a man DRESSED like a clown!"

I asked Grannie if Granddad was getting enough exercise. She said: "Who, him? He reckons tossing and turning in bed is enough exercise for anyone."

Recently my grandson's teacher was complimenting him on his work and asked, "Who do you take after?"

My grandson replied, "That's easy. I take after my grandfather — he used to be intelligent."

grandbaby around the finger of a grandfather. — Joy Hargrove

Felicity, aged three, asked me why she hadn't got a granddad. I explained to her that he had gone to Heaven. "I suppose you'll be next," said Felicity in a matter-of-fact little voice.

The four-year-old granddaughter stared intently at her granddad's bald pate:

"Granddad, you haven't been eating your crusts."

Gran says about a know-all: She thinks herself clever but she can't make the clock strike more than once.

Grandma came to our house and told me off because of the state of my bedroom, but her comment made us all laugh. She said: "If you'd only tidy your room every day, you wouldn't have to do it so often."

Every generation revolts against its fathers and

"Grandpa, were you in the first war?"
"No, I hadn't been born."
"Were you in the second war?"
"No, I wasn't old enough."
Short pause for thought. "Couldn't you go out and start one?"

I called on Gran to tell her that an old friend of hers had gone to hospital to have a leg amputated.

"Nay, you don't say," she declared. "D'ye mean her foot an' all?"

When my four—year—old grandson came to visit me I asked how was Sunday School. He replied: "Not so good, Gran. You see, Daniel's in the lions' den again."

makes friends with its grandfathers. — Lewis Mumfordon

My grandfather was a joker; we had lots of laughs with him. He was very happy with Grandma but never sent her a birthday card — just gave her money to buy herself something she liked. She enjoyed this bit of extra cash and also wandering round the market. One Valentine's Day she received a card unsigned. She asked Granddad if he had sent it. A loud "No" was his reply, "You should know by now I'm not a sender of cards," keeping a serious face and continuing reading the morning paper (he had sent it). But he was adamant and kept his secret. Grandma wasn't at all pleased because what follows wasn't very romantic or flattering. The card showed rather a large lady wearing a very large hat with feathers, and the card read, 'I don't like the hat and darling, you are getting fat'. Recently Grandma bought a new hat for a forthcoming family wedding. We had some laughs, much to Grandma's annoyance. He still would not admit anything. She finally let the matter drop — but did wear the hat for my wedding.

Doris Kitching

I asked my five-year-old granddaughter if she liked school. She replied: "Well, I'll be glad when I leave this school and go to college."

One day a little girl was sitting and watching her mother do the dishes at the kitchen sink. She suddenly noticed that her mother had several strands of white hair sticking out in contrast on her brunette head.

She looked at her mother and inquisitively asked, "Why are some of your hairs white, Mum?"

Her mother replied, "Well, every time that you do something wrong and make me cry or unhappy, one of my hairs turns white."

The little girl thought about this revelation for a while and then said, "Mummy, how come ALL of Grandma's hairs are white?"

There's no place like home except Grandma's.

At a christening, the proud dad asked the new grandfather,
"And who do you think he's like, me or his mother?"
To which the grandfather replied cautiously, "That is difficult
to say until intelligence dawns upon that innocent face. At
present he is remarkably like both of you."

Missing Granddad

My gran smells of lavender soap
And has a face full of wrinkles,
And eyes like small, black shining beads.
Her hair is like silver thread
And her hands are as soft as a bed of feathers,
And when she's with Mum, she talks a lot.

My gran uses a teabag three times,
And saves bits of soap in a jar,
And collects old newspapers and plastic bags,
And rubber bands and safety pins.
"Waste not, want not," she says,
And when I visit, she laughs a lot.

My gran wears thick brown stockings
And slippers with holes in
And a colourerd scarf with a little silver brooch.
She keeps a photo of Granddad
On the old brown dresser,
And when she's alone, I think she cries a lot.

Gran told me she'd been to see her neighbour in hospital. "That were a waste o' time, and no mistake; she died the next day."

I took Grandma to a well-known department store which had a large cosmetics counter, as she'd said she wanted some perfumed soap. After curling up her nose at several bars she asked the young assistant the cost of one. To my embarrassment Grandma replied: "Ee lass, I'd want a new face for that price, not just a clean one."

When I was very young I broke a saucer at my Gran's house. Gran said, "You've broken your granddad's best saucer. What ever will he say when he has to drink out of his cup?" Mum and Gran chuckled but it wasn't until years later that I understood what was funny.

A man at sixty begins to realise that his grandfather was not so old

My gran collected eggs on the farm where my granddad worked and was allowed to keep the cracked ones. "Get many?" I asked her one day. She looked at me with a glint in her eyes and whispered, "Now, Denise, what's easier to crack than eggs?"

One of Granddad's favourite weather sayings when he couldn't get out to the allotment was: "If that there rain had 'a' bin snow it'd be six foot deep by now."

Mum and I laughed when we overheard Gran's conversation with an old friend she'd met while we were shopping. Her friend told her she was going into a certain hospital for a minor operation. Gran said: "Ah, that's a good hospital. My husband died there."

when he dies at eighty. — Sydney Smith, Canon of St Paul's, 1800

Gran was a real old Westmorland woman and had some quaint phrases. I particularly remember her saying, "There's nowt like a good laugh. It opens ivry pore in your carry-on."

My twin grandsons came to stay one weekend. I put them to bed but a few minutes later I could hear arguing. I asked what the matter was and Tim said: "It's Tom, he wants half the bed."

"But that's only fair," I said.

"But Tom wants his half in the middle, Gran."

My Irish grandmother, on meeting my future husband, remarked that, "He is clearly an educated man for he lifts his trousers at the knees before sitting down."

"If grandmas hadn't existed, kids would have

Harry did not want to have his face washed. Grandma explained that she had washed her face three times a day ever since she was a little girl. Harry looked at her face and merely said: "Yes, Granny, and look how it's shrunk."

When I told Granddad about our trip to the Lake District he said: "There's nowt there but scenery."

The teacher, giving a health talk to her class, warned them never to fondle animals.

"Can you give me an instance of the dangers of this, Jackie?" she asked.

"Yes, Miss, my grannie used to kiss her dog."

"And what happened?"

"It died."

My gran used to call the midwife "a bairn-catcher".

inevitably invented them." — Doug Larson

I was told this tale by my mother. During the war, Gran jumped from her bed when the air-raid siren sounded. She could not switch on the light for fear of piercing the blackout and her fingers scratched across the bedside table in a frantic search.

"What are you looking for?" inquired Granddad.

"My false teeth," she replied.

"Nay," he said, "never mind your teeth. They're dropping bombs, not pork pies."

Granddad always used to criticise Grandma's baking. He once said of her pastry: "You could shoe hosses wi' it!"

My gran wasn't a great one for housework. When I mentioned that the sideboard needed polishing, she said, "In this house, love, dust is a noun and not a verb."

Just when I got my life organsed I became a grandparent.

My grandson told me that the dog had eaten a chocolate bar he had left on the table. "That's very naughty of him." I said.

"I know, but it's all right," said my grandson, "because I've eaten one of his biscuits to teach him a lesson."

Gervase Phinn

Grampa Bentley

My grandpa is old now.
His head is as bald as a hard-boiled egg
But inside millions of things are going on.
My grandpa is old now,
But when he sneezes
He blows the leaves off the trees.
My grandpa is old now,
But when he walks
His legs go snip-snap like a pair of scissors.
My grandpa is old now,
But when he smiles
The sun comes out and the birds sing.
My grandpa is old now.
But he doesn't act his age.

ELIZABETH PHINN (AGED SEVEN)

When I visited my grandparents Gran would often be reading while Gramps snoozed in his chair. I once asked Gramps why he didn't also read. "Well," he said, "it takes all the pleasure out of it when you have to wear glasses, doesn't it? And anyway, your Gran tells me all t' tale when she's finished — whether I like it or not."

Grandma said the doctor told her she was a maniac. It took us a while to realise he'd actually said she was anaemic.

Grandma talking about marriage (loudly enough so Granddad could hear): "Afore you get wed he'll lift you over a puddle but after, he'll not look round if you've fallen in the beck."

Grandparents are the footsteps to the future.

Grandparents and technology

My granddad puts 'the' in front of anything to do with the web: "The Google isn't working today", "Your mum signed me up for the Facebook but I don't like it".

Gran: "Close the door, you're letting the WiFi out!"

Me: "Grandma, you've got your caps lock on, turn it off."
Gran: "That's so I can see what I'm typing."

Grandma: "Do they deliver e-mails on Sunday?"

My grandma seems to think you are supposed to hold a mobile phone like a walkie talkie when you talk, bringing it down in front of her mouth to speak. With her also being a bit hard of hearing she shouts down it as well, giving the impression she's in the middle of a battlefield.

Gramps: "My computer has a virus. What if it kills me?"

"But how did you know I was here?" said my gran, answering her mobile while at her friend's house, forgetting that mobile phones are not tethered to your home.

Gran: "What does this smiley mean?"

Grandma, typing on a Facebook page: "Facebook please put pictures from Christmas on here."
Me: "Grandma, what are you talking about?"
Grandma: "Am trying to put the pictures from Christmas on the Facebook but it won't work."
Me: "LOL!! Were you trying to command it like a robot?"
Grandma: "Your granddad told me to try it."

My gran tried to rewind a DVD once she'd finished it like you had to do with VCR, because she wanted to make sure it was ready for the next person who watches it.

When I built my first PC, my grandparents thought shutting down was called downloading. So, when it was time for bed, my gran would always ask me to download. I found this hilarious and never corrected them. To this day, my grandparents still think it's the correct terminology.

On being congratulated at the time of his golden wedding anniversary on the continued beauty of the woman he had married, Granddad replied: "Oh, I never took any notice of that; can she cook and will she grumble is all I ever asked myself." Grandma was not amused.

Grandma always had a nice turn of phrase. Talking about two tall and thin sisters who walked past her window: "They look like two geraniums in a back window."

Grandma says she was often embarrassed by my late Grandpa, especially when they were out together, as he could be very abrupt. One day when they were having lunch in a café he complained about the burnt pastry on his pie, saying to the waitress: "I don't mind eating horse-flesh but I don't want t' horse's collar an' all!"

Commenting on a spoon left standing in the teacup,

Grandma talking to her friend: "It seemed like my body was totally out of shape, so I got my doctor's permission to join a fitness club and start exercising. I decided to take an aerobics class for seniors. I bent, twisted, gyrated, jumped up and down, and perspired for an hour. But by the time I got my leotards on the class was over."

Granddad, talking to a friend: "I've had two bypass surgeries, a hip replacement, new knees, fought prostate cancer and diabetes. I'm half blind, can't hear anything quieter than a jet engine, take 40 different medications that make me dizzy, winded, and subject to blackouts. Have bouts with dementia. Have poor circulation, hardly feel my hands and feet any more. I can't remember if I'm 85 or 92. Have lost all my friends. But, thank God, I still have my driver's licence."

Gran says: "That's how Nelson lost his eye."

I told my four grandchildren that there was a dragon living in the outhouse (previously the outside toilet). Actually there was paint stripper inside as well as weed killer, so I needed them to stay out. I even used to get my neighbour to bring me coal for the dragon's snacks. But my plan backfired as the children told all the locals they met about the dragon and for months afterwards lots of youngsters were forever daring each other to take a look inside. In the end I had to lock the dragon's den!

Grandmother
My grandmother, travelling in Spain,
Fell from a fast-moving train,
She bounced down the track,
And when she climbed back,
Exclaimed, "Could I do that again?"

About the visit of a disliked relation Gran says: "She's

> Gran had a habit of saying the wrong word.
> Once we were talking about the guards at
> Buckingham Palace and she said: "Are they the
> ones who wear bosoms on their heads?"

We giggled when we overheard Grannie on the phone to her friend saying: "Oh, I didn't know you didn't know. If I'd known you didn't know I would have told you …"

On seeing a very thin person, my Gran would say, "I've seen more fat on a tinker's bike."

I asked Granddad if he was going to the annual agricultural fair. He replied: "Nah, it's always the same year after year after year. I haven't been for forty years now."

---

about as welcome as haemorrhoids are to a jockey."

"Now come along Andrew, you tell Grandpa where you
buried his car keys."

I was taking my nine-year-old grandson around Conisborough Castle.

"That's called a portcullis," I told him as we entered the stronghold.

"It's an iron gate, Gramps," Harry replied.

"I know," I said, "but it's called a portcullis."

"I don't think so."

All the way around the castle Harry persisted in maintaining that it was an iron gate.

In the gift shop I found a book with details of the castle and showed him a picture of the entrance with the word 'portcullis' above it.

"There, you see," I told my grandson, perhaps rather smugly. "It is a portcullis, as I told you."

Gran says: "The tea's so strong you could trot a mouse across it."

He thought for a moment. "You know, Gramps," he said after a while, "the really annoying thing about you is that you always have to be right."

"When did you first decide that you wanted to be an author?" I was asked after my talk at a book festival. I cannot pinpoint the precise moment when I came to the decision that I wanted to be a writer but it was certainly on those occasions when I sat with my grandmother listening to her interesting stories and anecdotes, reminiscences and commentaries, that the seed was sown.

One most vivid early memory of mine of my Grandma was when she read with me. I say 'with me' rather than 'to me' for we would share the experience. She would stop on occasions in the reading to elaborate on the story or ask me about it, what I thought of the characters, what certain words meant or how the story might end.

Visiting her after church on Sunday, I would sit with her and she would open a large, hard-backed picture book of Old Testament stories and lift the text from the page in her soft Irish voice. The book was full of rousing accounts, vivid characters and many exciting events. It was always the Bible stories on Sunday. At other times she would read poetry: The Highwayman by Alfred Noyes, where 'the moon was a ghostly galleon tossed upon cloudy seas'; The Lake Isle of Innisfree by W B Yeats, with its 'bee-loud glade'; The Pied Piper of Hamlyn with those repulsive rodents; Matilda, who set the house on fire.

Grandma
I loved my Grandma.
She was very thoughtful.
Her hair was like silver
And her face like gold,
Eyes like emeralds
That glinted in the sun.
She was very precious.
AMY TALBOT (AGED SIX)

---

enough to take care of them. — Rita Rudner

When my Grandma read, I thrilled at the sound of the words, the rhythms and the rhymes and would sit goggle-eyed at the power of her voice and her extraordinary memory. She knew passages of verse by heart and had a natural feel for measure and stress.

As an older child I would take along with me on my visits the book of the moment and it was my turn to read to her: *Kidnapped* or *White Fang*, *Moonfleet* or *Children of the New Forest*, *King Solomon's Mines* or *Treasure Island*.

One favourite was Swiss Family Robinson with its garish coloured plates and big print. I loved the story where all the members of the shipwrecked family work happily together under the benign guidance of a father who was both strong and wise and who sported bulging muscles and a long chestnut beard.

It was my Grandma Mullarkey who bought me my first dictionary when I started secondary school and the

Grandparents are the most precious kind of antiques.

The reason grandchildren and grandparents get along so well is that they have a common enemy.

treasured portable Olivetti typewriter with the black and red ribbon. I would sit with it on my lap feeling like 'a real writer'.

Grandma Mullarkey opened a door in my early childhood and changed my life for the better and when she died she left a great gap. When I was sixteen I accompanied my mother to Doncaster Gate Hospital where my grandmother, aged 81, was dying of stomach cancer. There is no image in my childhood that I carry with me more clearly than the one of my grandmother in the hospital bed. She looked pale and weary propped up, clutching her rosary beads, but her eyes were as bright and intelligent as ever. She told me not to look so miserable. "Remember," she said, "a smile will gain you ten years of life."

Now, as grandparent myself, I take down from the bookshelf that large, hard-backed picture book of Old Testament stories which belonged to my grandmother to read with my grandchildren, and in doing so I am reminded

A zest for life is one of the most important examples

of the wonderful woman with the shining eyes and soft
voice who gave me my love of books and reading.

Letter to Grannie and Grampa

Dear Grannie and Grampa,
Mother's come out in a rash
And Father's got the mumps,
Richard, he's got tummy ache
And Dominic's got lumps.
Lizzie, she's got chicken pox,
And the dog is full of fleas,
The poor old cat's back from the vets
With an unexplained disease.
But you'll be pleased to hear, I know
That there's nothing wrong with me,
And I cannot wait for Sunday
When you're coming round for tea.

---

a grandparent can pass on to their grandchildren.

One of my granddad's 'tall tales' involved the large bullet that was displayed on the chimney breast above the open coal fire in his living room. It was a souvenir of his wartime service in the Royal Navy when he was stationed in and around Scapa Flow. Working aboard wooden-bottomed minesweepers designed to avoid sonar detection by German submarines was a risky occupation, resulting in him being sunk at least three times. But more dangerous still was the way in which he claimed to have collected his memento — he reckoned to have caught it in his teeth while under fire from an enemy fighter plane.

Many years later a visitor told him that the bullet had not been correctly de-commissioned and, to all intents and purposes, it was still live. Needless to say, it was promptly removed from its position above the fire.

Tim Gray

Gran phoned us to say she'd got herself a new dog. She said it was a cross between a golden cockerel and a Spaniard!

We try to be really truthful to our grandchildren — for example, we won't sugar coat what we say if people or animals die. They'll get the best explanations we can give to them in a kind way. However, after one particularly unruly visit I told them they've got a cousin who lives in the loft, and if they're not good I'll send them to live with her. I got a real telling off from my daughter (their mother!).

Granddad had some fine old sayings. One which I still ponder over is: "There's nowt worse than slack pants, loose boots and a cap that doesn't fit."

Gran says: "If you ask me, talking is overrated."

Granddad drew his chair up beside Gran's sewing machine and began a series of comments: "Don't you think it's running too fast? You need to look out or you'll have the needle through your finger."

"What on earth's the matter with you?" demanded Gran angrily. "I've been running this machine for years."

"Oh," retorted the husband, "I was only trying to help you sew as you often help me to drive the car."

Grandfather had some quaint and often crude phrases. When he tried to cut the Sunday joint with a blunt knife he would say: "You could ride to London and back bare—arsed on this knife."

"I hear you're thinking of keeping monkeys," said Grandma when I visited her. I told her she must be mistaken but she insisted that's what my mother had told her. When I saw

Grandmother-grandchild relationships are simple. Grandmas

my mother I asked her about this and she giggled, saying:
"I told her you were going to buy an apiary!"

Gran got some new false teeth and I asked her
how they were: "I've to take them out for
eating, like, but for going to t' shops and bingo
they're champion."

My grandfather was something of a wit. One evening in the
local public house he examined his pint of beer prior to
taking a gulp.

"Looks like rain," observed the landlord.

"Aye, and it tastes like it too," replied my grandfather.

Gramps never really learned to read and write but he
tried his best. On the gate of his smallholding he put
up a sign: 'For sail – weak old chicks'.

---

are short on criticism and long on love.

My gran was describing how she had a 'locust preacher' staying at her home one Sunday. I said, "You've got the wrong word Gran, it's 'local' preacher, not 'locust'. Locusts are the creatures that eat up everything in front of them."

"Why then, it's t' same thing," she replied. "For yon chap eyt up everything I set afore 'im all reight!"

My grandson hasn't quite got a grasp of spoken English yet. When I asked him when he was due to start school, he replied: "A good bit since yet." Realising he hadn't got that right he tried again with: "A long time since now."

When Grannie went for a blood test, the nurse asked if she knew her type. Grannie responded with: "Aye, I'm the passionate type."

The sign of old age is to extol the past at the expense of

Hearing that Granddad had reached the age of a hundred, the reporter interviewed my Grandma on the subject. "You must be very proud of him," he remarked.

"Oh, I don't know," was the unexpected reply. "The only thing he's ever done is grow old, and he's taken a mighty long time over that."

I had to giggle the first time my four—year—old grandson saw a man leading a horse by a length of rope: "Oh look Grannie, that man's horse has broken down!"

I took Granddad for dinner at my sister's house where we had stew and dumplings. On the way home I said to him, "Those dumplings were a bit sad, weren't they?" to which he quickly replied, "Sad? Poor things, they were damn near heartbroken."

---

the present. — Sydney Smith, Canon of St Paul's, 1800

Of an overdressed woman wearing a fancy hat, my granddad, a former farmer, would remark: "She looks like my old heifer with all her show rosettes on."

Granddad was always blunt. I remember just after I'd got married asking him to sample my first attempt at making strawberry jam.

"Well, what do you think of it?" I asked.

"It lacks something," he replied.

"What?"

"Flavour, I think."

All the Time in the World
My granddad never hurries.
He walks and walks ever so slowly,
And plods along,
And ambles and strolls.
He has all the time in the world.
Mums rush, Dads dash,
But Granddad never hurries.

Gran says: "When I think of my childhood I'm filled with neuralgia."

On the Sunday before my first day at Low Valley Infants I was whirling around in a state of what people from Muker call 'Reeth Giddiness' and people from Reeth call 'Muker Jumpiness'. My mother and dad decided to take me and my brother to see my grandma in Great Houghton to calm me down. She was renowned for her coconut cakes; for their consistency, which was like that of a breeze block, and their taste, which was like that of CS gas.

We got to her house and she said to me and my brother, "I know what you lads would like: some lovely coconut cake," gesturing at a charred and smoking cinder on the table. We tried to escape, running out of the back door past my mother's despairing grasp, and we scaled the wall at the back of Grandma's yard, running along bricks as solid as her cakes. I slipped. I slipped like an Olympic skater in a final and crashed to the ground and hit my head and knocked myself daft. Stars whirled round my head as though I was in *The Dandy*.

And that's why I started school three days late. 'School in the morning' meant Wednesday for me. And that's why I've always been three days behind. It was the coconut cake that set me back!

Ian McMillan

Grandma returned home after shopping one day and told Granddad she had got a marvellous bargain at an auction sale. It was a brass name-plate inscribed: 'Dr John Smith'.

Granddad asked why on earth she'd bought it. Gran replied, "Well, I might be a widow some day, and I might marry a Dr John Smith — then this would come in handy."

Grandma had a saying which has stayed with me all my life: "The less a chap knows, the prouder he is of his knowledge."

Granddad played the French horn in the village band for many years. He recently moved into a town and joined the band there so I asked him how he was getting on. "There's nowt to it," he declared. "They only let me blow when t' conductor wags his stick at me. Back in t' village I played every note fro' start to finish."

When a child is born, so are grandmothers. — Judith Levy

Grannie describing Grandpa's weight loss: "He was so thin I could hardly find him in bed. He was just like a crease in the blanket."

When Granddad celebrated his ninetieth birthday I asked him what was his recipe for so long a life.

"Contentment," he replied.

"So you have had a contented and happy life, no domestic troubles?" I asked.

"None at all. You see, when your gran starts to natter I go into the garden shed and if I get mad with her she goes in the kitchen."

A favourite saying of my Gran when talking about a local gossip was "Aye, she's one o' that sort that goes looking for lice i' bald heads."

When grandparents enter the door, discipline

We invited Granddad to tea. He was always reluctant to try new food but I offered him some gorgonzola cheese, and he took a piece. After a close inspection, he put it in his mouth, chewed it, and spat it out.

"Have you never tasted it before?" I asked.

"No, never tasted such stuff afore," was the reply, "but I've trod in it!"

Granddad liked a little flutter on the horses. "Did you pick a slow one, Granddad?" I'd ask when his horse lost. He'd reply: "Ah wouldn't say he was slow, lad, but t' jockey took a packed lunch wi' him."

My grandparents lived in an old millworker's cottage in need of a bit of TLC. Every time anyone left the house, Grandma would tell them: "Mind the step cos it ain't there, and don't forget that the bottom one is the last!"

---

flies out the window. — Ogden Nash

When I asked Gran why Gramps hadn't come with us to visit an auntie, she said: "He won't sit around in other people's draughts. He'd rather stay at home where he knows where they all come from."

An old Yorkshirewoman was celebrating her birthday with her family. Proud of her longevity, she went on at great length about her good health, and remarked that she was thinking about bequeathing her body to medical science. Finally her granddaughter lost patience and exclaimed: "Nay, Grandma, you're not going to do us out of a ham tea after ninety years."

Small boy when asked about his grandfather's age: "Well, I don't right know but he's been around the house for as long as I can remember."

You do not really understand something unless

On seeking career advice from my Yorkshire Grandpa he told me: "If tha wants to be happy in life, lass, do summat tha likes doing. If tha wants to be even happier, get somebody to pay thee to do it."

Gramps didn't like fussy shop assistants. Once, in a men's department in Harrogate, he was asked by a gushing assistant: "What is sir's pleasure?"

Gramps replied harshly, "Greyhound racing, pigeons and rugby league. Now get me a cap."

My gran trying to explain to me that she and her twin are not alike: "My sister and me we ain't no more alike than if we wasn't us. Yes, she's just as different as me, only the other way."

---

you can explain it to your grandmother. — Proverb

Granddad had the devil in him. He was always in the pub and was once admonished by the vicar who'd spotted him at the bar when he called in to see the landlord: "You should read the Bible," he told Granddad.

"I 'ave read t' Bible," Granddad replied.

"Well, didn't that discourage you from drinking?" said the vicar.

Granddad took another drink of beer before saying: "No, but it did discourage me from reading."

When I told Grandma, who'd lived all her life in a small village on the lonely moors of North Yorkshire, that I was going to college in London, she said: "Well if there's anything you can't find there, let me know and I'll get it for you from t' village shop."

Grandfathers are for loving and mending things.

I was sitting at my dressing table, putting some lipstick on and getting ready to go to a local WI meeting. My granddaughter, Amy, aged six, was combing my hair. "Can't find any nits, yet, Grannie," she announced proudly.

My old grandma, at 80-odd, used to walk from Patrington in the East Riding to Sunk Island and spend the day with us. She used to wear long black flowing skirts and tops with an inset of lace pinned in the V-neck with tiny gold safety pins. She only had one eye, we loved her and she could make us giggle at midday lunch; she would say:

> I eats mi peas
> wi' honey
> I've dun it all mi life.
> Makes the peas
> Taste funny
> But it sticks 'em
> To mi knife.

Then at tea-time it was always:

> Pass the tarts Mrs Hart.
> No thank you Mrs Bonham
> I'm none too fond on 'em.

Pat Souter, Grimsby

I phoned Grannie and during the conversation I asked how Gramps was doing.

"Oh, I hardly know. He's so busy in his shed I only see him for about an hour a day," she said.

"Oh, I am sorry," I replied.

She replied quickly: "Oh, that's all right. The hour soon passes."

I usually did a little bit of shopping for my old gran when I visited her. I asked her once if she wanted her usual 2 oz of cheese. She replied: "Get me 4 oz then I shall have some when I ain't got none."

When a Yorkshire granddad was told by his doctor to cut back on eating and have a simpler diet, he objected strongly: "Ah'm not gunna starve missen to death for t' sake o' livin' a few years longer!"

Gran says about a boaster: "Aye, all her eggs are double-yolked."

When I Am Old

"My grannie wobbles, you know," said the child.
"She's very old, you see, and has an illness.
It makes her tremble so and shake her head
And sometimes says things we don't understand.
We wheel her round the garden in her chair,
And help her with her tea and wipe her mouth,
And sometimes comb her soft and silvery hair.
It has a special name, my Grannie's illness.
'Old Timer's Disease' they call it."

If, when I am old and trembling and I shake my head,
And someone helps me with my tea,
And wipes my mouth and combs my silvery hair,
Please let them say I have 'Old Timer's Disease'.
It's rather warm and comforting I think.

A grandam's name is little less in love than is the

Our family was by no means well off, but my Grandma Mullarkey managed the small amount of money meticulously. There were five children to feed. She would shop judiciously and was always on the look-out for a bargain. My mother once told me about visiting the fish counter at Sheffield Castle Market when she was aged around six. Grandma, looking elegant in her Sunday best, asked for one piece of fish (for Granddad) and any fish heads, which she would use to make the most delicious soup. "For the cat," she told the fishmonger.

"We haven't got a cat," my mother piped up with all the honesty of a young child.

"Yes, we have," said Grandma, giving her a knowing look and a wink.

"No, we haven't," persisted my mother to all in earshot.

---

doting title of a mother. — William Shakespeare

"My mother boils up the fish heads in a big pan over the fire for our tea."

I was playing with my four-year-old grandson and his race-car set. After telling him several times not to do a certain thing, I yelled at him to stop. He came over to me with a long face, head down and lower lip quivering. He said, "I still like you, Granddad, but if you talk to me like that again, you may not be able to play with my race-car set any more."

On holiday in France with my son, his wife and their small daughter Megan, I started packing the case for the return journey home. I decided to slip in a couple of extra bottles of wine between my clothes. My granddaughter must have heard her father telling me that to put the wine in would make me over the limit for duty-free goods and I could get into trouble. Going through customs my granddaughter

A grandfather is someone with silver in his hair and gold in his heart.

watched intently as the official opened my case and began checking my luggage. As he reached into the bottom of my case Megan said in a whisper loud enough for all the hear, "He's getting warm now, isn't he, Grandpa?"

My grandfather, a farmer, always maintained that "manure in your land is like sugar in your tea".

Granddad was proud of the wonderful display of flowers in his front garden. When visitors saw his roses and dahlias they would ask him how he grew such large blooms. His answer was "Manure! Plenty of manure!"

Then when visitors saw his vegetable garden they would ask, "How do you grow such large turnips and cabbages?" His answer, as always, was "Manure! Plenty of manure!"

One day Grandma and I were standing near him as he

talked to some admiring passers-by. "It's all down to manure," he told them when they commented on the magnificent flowers. "Manure! Plenty of manure!"

"I do wish Granddad would say fertiliser to the visitors, instead of manure," I commented.

Grandma turned round to me and said, "You leave him alone. It took me twenty years to get him to say manure."

I took my granddaughter, Bethany, aged twelve, for a meal at a rather posh restaurant in town. On the menu it said that meals for children under twelve would be half price.

Always one for a good deal, I told the waitress when she asked that my granddaughter was eleven.

"No, I'm not, Grannie!" cried Bethany. "I'm twelve."

"Ah, yes," I said, "of course you are." Then, looking at the waitress and feeling rather embarrassed by my fib, I told

---

and your money the last thing you part with."

her. "It was her birthday yesterday."

"No it wasn't, Grannie," said Bethany. "My birthday was last July."

"Yes, of course, dear," I said. "Silly me."

My granddaughter looked at the waitress, shook her head and sighed. "Old age," she said.

Grandma commenting on the ballet: "They were hopping about like frogs that had been trodden on."

After putting my grandchildren to bed, I changed into my old slacks and a droopy blouse, took off my make-up and started to wash my hair. I heard the children getting rowdy so I threw a towel around my head and stormed into their room, putting them back to bed with stern warnings. As I left the room, I heard the youngest child say, "Who was THAT?"

On the seventh day God rested. His grandchildren

Granddad, commenting on the death of a lazy neighbour: "Well he must've rusted cos he's not worn away."

I took my grandchildren to a well-known fast-food chain for lunch but the pair couldn't make up their minds about what they wanted to eat. Finally, I grinned at the waitress and said, "Oh, just bring them bread and water."

One of the boys looked up at me with sad eyes and said quietly, "Grandpa, can I have ketchup on mine?"

My grandson was visiting one day when he asked, "Grandma, do you know how you and God are alike?"

I mentally polished my halo while I asked, "No, how are we alike?"

"You're both old," he replied.

must have been out of town. — Gene Perret

My wife remembers her grandmother sitting in a deckchair in front of a hired tent in Bridlington. Grandma was wearing her winter coat and a hat. In a photo we have she looks like a cross between Grandma in the Giles' cartoons and Geronimo. Once settled, out would come what was left of the egg sandwiches, now with that unique added ingredient — sand.

Occasionally my cousin and I rode in the back of my granddad's Austin, which had leather seats. I don't think Grandma Clara was quite as daft as she made out, but I personally heard her come out with those two classics: "Aren't there a lot of places called 'Loose Chippings'," and "That truck's come a long way, all the way from Bedford". She once had a pet whippet but it ran away and she wasn't fast enough to catch it.

My grandfather Art loved Brid. Just like my wife's lot, we'd find our own section of beach and mark our territory with the indispensable canvas windbreaks. We changed from looking like a wagon train into something resembling a Bedouin encampment. Art always bought a carton of fresh winkles. He had his own pearl-topped winkle pin. He'd probe into a shell, spear a morsel of something that looked disgusting and eat it.

His wife, Grandma Clara by this time would usually be indulging in her habit of absent-mindedly flicking in and out her top set of dentures.

Richard Maulson

The worst thing a grandparent can do is to offer advice on the rearing of grandchildren. Grandparents, of course, may be right that children should mind their manners, not be fussy about their food, behave themselves, go to bed when they are told, not answer back, tidy their rooms but however well meant it is, young parents will not appreciate such 'helpful' advice from their own parents. The best thing grandparents can do is bite their tongues.

Elspeth Williams

When her Grandpa came to see my small daughter she suddenly looked up at him and said: "Were you in the Ark, Grandpa, when the flood came?"

"Oh no," said Grandpa, taken aback.

"Then why weren't you drowned, Grandpa?" asked my daughter severely.

I was walking with my grandson when I pointed and said, "Ooo look, a French poodle." He thought for a while before asking, "How did you know that dog was French?"

One day I looked after my two grandsons, ages six and three, while my daughter had her hair done. When she arrived home the six-year-old told her how beautiful she looked. Then he looked back at me and said, "And Gramma, you look almost beautiful."

About a lazy person, Gran says: "He'll never get

My three-year-old grandson once asked me, "Grandma, how old are you?"
"How old do you think I am?" I asked.
"Ten. I think you are ten."
"No," I said. "I'm sixty years old."
"Sixty?!" he replied. "I don't know THAT number."

My four-year-old grandson was looking at a photo album with his mum, when he saw a picture of her taken while she was pregnant. He asked her why she was so big and she told him that he was in her tummy. He looked from the picture to her tummy several times, before saying, "Mummy, did you swallow me?"

I asked my grandson to tell me his full name. He replied: "Daniel Peter Watson Come Here Now."

killed with work — unless it tumbles on top of him."

My grandson came to stay and so I gave him some paper and a pencil to draw with. Later, all I saw on his paper were two upright thick lines and one thin straight line linking them. Pointing at the picture, he told me, "That's a post and that's a post and that's a washing line."

"But where is the washing?" I asked.

Back came the quick reply, "Mum hasn't done it yet."

I asked Gran if she liked my flashy new dress. She thought for a minute before saying: "Well, put it this way, when I come into a room I want people to ask 'who is she?' not 'who does she think she is?'."

"My granddad's just been to the dentist and got a new set of teeth," said little Johnny proudly.

His friend, looking very interested, replied: "What are they going to do with the old ones?"

Gran says of a useless man: "As much use as ashtrays on a motorbike."

Johnny looked thoughtful. "I suppose they'll save them and cut them down for Dad," he said.

Rather sarcastically, I said to my grandson when he visited: "Your hands are very clean today for a change. What has happened, John?"
   "Oh, I've been practising whistling with my fingers, Gran," was the reply.

As I look back to my childhood days, I often wonder how I could have been so gullible! But, when with Granddad it was so easy. He could convince me to do anything. I believed everything he told me, because I believed in him.

Sometimes I wonder if I knew the pot eggs that he told me to sit upon were pot and would never hatch. Or if I pretended not to know just to please him.

Janette Hamer

A grandma washed her baking tins, then left them in the hearth to dry. When her four-year-old grandson asked why, he was told that it stopped them going rusty. Next day the child had a bath, and was being dried in front of the fire when the vicar came.

"Getting dried where it's warm?" asked the vicar.

"I have to," replied the little chap. "It stops me going rusty."

Our small granddaughter had been given a bicycle for Christmas. Some days later our local garage manager told me she had brought it in to see if he could stop some of the rattles it made when she rode it. "You know," she told him solemnly, "Santa Claus doesn't make things the way he used to."

Grandparents make the world a little softer, a little kinder, a little warmer.

Grandma, a farmer's wife, once described my haircut as "calf-licked on both sides".

Grandma and Granddad lived a cat-and-dog life and had not spoken to each other for years. In course of time Granddad fell ill and lay dying. Grandma, anxious for a reconciliation before it was too late, decided to make the first advance.

She went upstairs to his bedside and, breaking the long, long silence, said: "Albert, where do you want to be buried?"

The answer came back without hesitation and in a voice full of malice: "On top of thee."

I was in town with my grandparents and as we passed a very posh confectionery shop, Granddad stopped and pointed at some expensive buns, saying that we should buy some.

Quick as a flash after looking at the price, Grandma said, "Them's not for folk like us that eats with our elbows on the table."

The teacher said, "One day, Carlie, the wind will change and your face will stay like that!"

"That's what my Grannie says," said the little girl when she was told off for sulking.

My own grandmother's use of English would have fascinated the connoisseur of the colloquial; she had a rich variety of speech often possessed by the Irish — lively, colourful and vibrant — and shared with her three daughters an acerbic turn of phrase when speaking of those she disliked.

Her comments on the failings and the unfortunate appearances of others were never mordacious or malicious because in their humour there was a sort of warmth and the listener could not help but smile. Her idioms were legendary in the family:

Talking about a ham-fisted workmate, Gran says:

She's that good, she bites the altar rails;
He has eyes like a couple of cold, fried eggs;
She has a mouth like a torn pocket;
He's as much use as a grave robber in a crematorium;
If she died with that face on her, nobody'd wash the corpse;
It runs in the family like Kitty O'Hara's nose;
A shut mouth catches no flies;
He's so fond of work, he'd lie down beside it;
She has an expression like last year's rhubarb.

I once took a friend to see her, a boy with red hair and very prominent front teeth. "Poor lad," commiserated my grandmother, "that young fellow could eat a tomato through a tennis racket."

On another occasion, on seeing a particularly fractious and unfortunate looking pair of twins creating havoc on a bus she was said to have remarked: "The mother, poor woman, would have been better off with a pair of jugs."

"He's about as much use as a yard of pump water."

Interrogation in the Nursery

Infant: What's that?

School Inspector: What?

Infant: That on your face.

School Inspector: It's a moustache.

Infant: What does it do?

School Inspector: It doesn't do anything.

Infant: Is it alive?

School Inspector: No, it's not alive.

Infant: Does it go up your nose?

School Inspector: No.

Infant: Could I have one?

School Inspector: No.

Infant: Why?

School Inspector: Little girls don't have moustaches.

Infant: Can I have one when I grow up?

School Inspector: No.

Infant: Why?

School Inspector: Ladies don't have them either.

Infant: Well my Grannie's got one.

If your baby is beautiful and perfect, never cries or fusses, sleeps on schedule and burps on demand, an angel all the time, you're the grandma.

I took Gran to an art exhibition in the local institute and we stood next to the proud artist as we admired one particular watercolour. Meaning to say that the painting was 'a sight for sore eyes' she actually commented, 'Ooh, that's quite an eyesore'! I've never been so embarrassed. We giggled about it all the way home and still talk about it years on.

I asked Grandma if Granddad was in Heaven. She replied: "Your Granddad will have pushed his way through t' pearly gates, while other folk just stood and stared at 'em!"

About a shallow person, Gran says: "Trouble with

When our cat was a kitten we took her to the vet to be spayed. I didn't want my grandson to worry about her having an operation (he was six at the time) so I said she was going to a party with her kitten friends. When we went to collect her she had a big bald patch on one side with stitches clearly showing so I told him she'd fallen off the bouncy castle.

Fast forward a few years and we took our then elderly cat to be put down, and I tried to soften it a bit by saying that once he'd died, he'd go up to the sky to be a star. This time my grandson informed me that stars are made out of gas, not cats, and I shouldn't be so stupid.

I was talking on the phone to my three-year-old grandson but I couldn't make out what he was saying so I kept asking, "What?" until finally, exasperated, he said, "Grandma, you're not listening loud enough!"

him is he talks in yards and thinks in inches."

I asked my granddaughter what she had done at the Brownie troop meeting. She said the leader had asked the girls what good deeds they had done at home since the last meeting. So I asked her what the girls had answered, and it seems they told of washing the floors, dusting the furniture and making the beds. I then asked my grandchild what she had done to help.

She looked solemn as she said, "I kept out of Mother's way."

Grandma didn't mince her words. When a neighbour popped in to see her she said:

"Go ahead, lass, an' hev another piece o' cake."

"No, thanks," was the reply. "I've had three already."

"Tha's hed four," said Grandma, "but you're welcome to another piece, lass."

Whenever I asked after Grandma's health, she would say:

I was brought up in a village and all five of my grandchildren grew up in the country. Although they'd come across animal death before I was a bit worried about what to say when, while driving two of the grandchildren in my car, I bumped into and killed a fox which was running across the road. As it happens, they were far less upset than I was, and the youngest told me off, saying I should drive more slowly and look out for animals on the country lanes.

When my grandson asked me how old I was, I teasingly replied, "I'm not sure."
"Look in your underwear, Granddad," he advised, "mine says I'm 4 to 6."

"Still kicking but not raising much dust."

My granddaughter asked me what happens when you die. I said I didn't know but that I liked to believe we went to live on clouds. I'd forgotten about that until later that year when we took her to the airport to wave her mum and dad off on a short break together while I babysat – cue screaming child who thought her parents were "heading into the clouds".

My granddad was a real tease and I was often laughed at when I repeated some of the things he'd told me (which I'd believed). He once told me that bacon grows on trees cos it's a type of vegetable; that eels are the hair from a horse's tail; that broccoli is actually a baby tree; that kidney beans are mouse kidneys and bollards are really baby lamp posts and will only grow into full-sized lamp posts if they are watered every day.

Of a pompous woman, Gran says: "She's no better than she should be."

Grandma used to tell us stories about being a waitress in a posh restaurant. One story involved a curt customer who always asked for one piece of toast, one egg, a pot of tea and a kind word.

One day Grandma delivered all but the last item. The pompous customer said: "Err, young lady, what about the kind word?"

Grandma inhaled sharply and raised her eyes to the ceiling before replying: "Don't eat that egg!"

When I was curator of the local museum I encouraged children to bring finds, always hoping something of importance would turn up. In came a little girl with three small stones in her hand. "What are these, dear?" I asked. "My grannie's gallstones," was the smiling reply.

Of a tight-fisted man, Gran says: "He wouldn't give a blind hen a worm."

Grandma posing by a palm,
Her sister resting on her arm,
My Auntie Alice by the door
Of her little village store,
Granddad sitting in a chair,
Looking young and debonair,
Painted backdropped country vista
With a potted aspidistra,
My mother, when a little girl,
In a dress designed to twirl,
Whiskered men I've never known,
Cousin Margaret on her own,
The chaise longue that she leans upon,
Symbolising times long gone,
And so I sit here leafing through,
Those pages now no longer new,
Precious mem'ries made to last,
By sepia moments from the past.

BRIAN H GENT

One day my grandson and I were out for a walk when we came to a very small churchyard. On the stone pillars of the gates was engraved AD1876, so I asked him what he thought this meant. He thought for a while and said: "AD — All dead, and there's eighteen-hundred-and-seventy-six of them."

"Now children," said the schoolmistress, "I want you all to make a nice Christmas card for your grandma."
    Up piped little Alfie: "Please Miss, I haven't got a grandma, but I've got an Aunt Elsie and she's just as good."

My grandson wished me happy birthday and asked how old I was. I told him, 68.
    My grandson was quiet for a moment, and then he asked, "Did you start at one?"

Blessed be the ties that bind generations.

I was staying at my granddaughter's for Christmas. My great grandchildren, a girl of nine, and a boy of six, had many presents and among the boy's presents was a mouth organ which he was trying to play.

I took it from him, explaining about "suck and blow" and also played him a few easy tunes.

It being Sunday I asked him if he knew any hymns. He replied: "I only know one hymn and that's three blind mice."

Children in my granddaughter's school had a history lesson on Mary, Queen of Scots, and her imprisonment at Bolton Castle. In an essay written after the lesson on the character of the unhappy Queen my granddaughter wrote: "She was very wilful as a girl and very cruel when she grew up. This was the result of having five step-mothers."

Gran says about a mean old man: "He's as tight as a tick's arse."

My grandpa, Richard Crawshaw, was a successful businessman and a footballer with Manchester City and Halifax Town. His eldest son Derryk (my Dad) died when I was twelve and my Grandpa assumed his duties for a short while.

My sister, Sheena, and I were budding ballerinas and we were in a show at Lowther Gardens, in Lytham St Annes. Grandpa picked us up in his beautiful Princess Vanden Plas. I remember it had an incredible polished walnut interior. We were en route to the show and going round a corner when the back door fell open with me hanging on to it. Somewhat alarmed, and pre seatbelt days, I hung on to it and went with it. "Help, Gramps!" I screamed, using the affectionate name we had for him.

He replied: "I can't stop now dear, I'm concentrating!"

I've never forgotten that. Obviously I managed to heave myself back in and lived to tell the tale.

Angela Stringer

When our daughter had a baby at Christmas, we told our other four-year-old grandson it must have come from Santa Claus. He wasn't impressed, saying: "Tommy next door got an electric railway and John's sister had a pony — and we've got this!"

I overheard a man telling the barber of the pleasures of being a grandfather. "Ah reckon there's nowt wrong wi' it. You pick up t' little un, play wi' it as long as you want, an' then when it cries you give it back."

When my granddaughter was two, I looked after her almost every day. That meant that I needed to follow through on the potty training she was getting at home. One day, while she was on the potty, I went in to check on her and said, "Don't forget to wipe!"

She said, "Oh, I did that first!"

_____

Commenting on a heavily-bearded man, Gran says:

A small grandchild overheard as she was in deep conversation with her little friend: "Well, my Daddy says my Grannie's past her sell-by date."

I didn't know if my granddaughter had learned her colours yet, so I tested her. I pointed out something and asked her what colour it was. She would tell me and always she was correct. But it was fun for me, so I continued. At last she headed for the door, saying sagely, "Grandma, I think you should try to figure out some of these yourself."

While looking after my granddaughter, I decided to teach her to sew. After I had gone through a lengthy explanation of how to thread the machine, she stepped back, put her hands on her hips, and said in disbelief, "You mean you can do all that, but you can't operate my Game Boy?"

"He looks like a rat peeping through a yard-brush."

Never let your granddaughter into the bathroom...

My granddaughter was watching me put on my make-up, as she'd done many times before. After I applied my lipstick and started to leave, she said, "But Gramma, you forgot to kiss the toilet paper goodbye." I will probably never put lipstick on again without thinking about kissing the toilet paper goodbye.

Little Jean was watching me spread cold cream on my face. "What's that for, Grandma?" she asked.
"It's to make me beautiful, dear," I replied.
Later she watched me remove the cream and whispered, "It didn't work, did it?"

My granddaughter was watching in fascination as I cleaned my false teeth in the bathroom. I explained that, unlike hers, mine weren't real and I had to take them out to wash them to keep them nice and fresh. She noticed a bar of Pears soap on the washbasin — the round, brown, transparent kind.
"Is that your tongue, Grannie?" she asked.

Hayley, my three-year-old granddaughter, came into the bathroom just in time to see me remove my false teeth. "Jeremy! Jeremy!" she screamed to her brother. "Come quickly, Nana is doing magic!"

I was talking with my granddaughter when she asked, "Did God make you, Granddad?"

"Yes, God made me," I said.

A few minutes later, she asked, "Did God make me too?"

"Yes," I said.

After a moment she concluded: "You know, Granddad, God's doing a lot better job lately."

"I don't need any encyclopaedia," my grandmother told the salesmen at her door. "I've got a husband inside and he knows everything."

Granddad, collecting his small granddaughter from school, asked her to take her schoolbag and coat out to the car. "You're not too old to carry things yourself, Granddad, you know," she replied pertly.

My great-granddaughter, Ruth Hannah, aged
five, informed me: "Gramps, you've got a beard."
"No, Ruth, I shave every morning."
"Yes, you have, it's up your nose."

Adults should be careful about the advice they proffer. At
the zebra crossing a granddad told his grandson, "Be
observant and learn to use your eyes." At dinner, the child
announced, "Granddad, why do you keep a bottle of
whiskey in your shed and hide your cigarettes and only
smoke them when Grannie isn't around?"

At midnight father returned hom from the
village dance. His daughter came in about 1am.
Mother returned a few minutes later and was
about to lock up when the daughter called out,
"Don't lock the door, Grandma isn't in yet!"

---

and they give you back a million poiunds worth of pleasure.

Grandparents

Grandparents bestow upon their grandchildren
The strength and wisdom that time
And experience have given them.
Grandchildren bless their grandparents
With a youthful vitality and innocence
That help them stay young at heart forever.
Together they create a chain of love
Linking the past with the future.
The chain may lengthen,
But it will never part ...

After getting through one of the most indigestible meals he had ever eaten, Granddad stood up, pushed back his chair and said: "I think I'm getting an ulcer."

Grandma was deep in a catalogue which had arrived that morning. Without looking up she replied: "Tha's getting nowt till I've got a new coat."

My grandfather, known locally as Captain Theakston, had returned from the Somme minus a limb, and one of my earlier memories is of grandfather's escapades with his tin leg. He rode a bicycle with a fixed wheel and minus one pedal, but rode devilishly, challenging the grandchildren to races through the town, most of which he won. I remember him as a stern, but kind, old man who had built Bellfield the family home, and that is where I grew up, living with my parents in the top quarter of what was actually a rather grand and manorial semi-detached, on the outskirts of town.

Paul Theakston, Brewer, Black Sheep

A Lesson in Love

(extract from The Little Village School *by Gervase Phinn)*

"Good morning, Miss Wilson," said the HMI, entering the classroom. "May I join you?"

"Yes, of course," replied the teacher. "This is Mr Steel, children."

"Good morning, Mr Steel. Good morning, everybody," chorused the children.

"Some of you may remember Mr Steel," Miss Wilson told the children.

A child with curly blond hair and rosy red cheeks raised her hand. "He's a suspector, Miss!" shouted Blossom. "He helped me when I was sick."

"I hope you're feeling better now," said the inspector.

Our greatest blessings call us Grandma and Granddad.

"Yes, I am," she said. "I was really sick, Miss, but I managed to get it all in my cardy."

"Thank you, Blossom," said the teacher. "I think we have heard quite enough about that. Now Mr Steel is really interested to see what we are doing this morning, children, and he would like to find out how you are all getting on. Who will tell our visitor what we are doing?"

A freckley-faced boy with large glasses raised a hand. "We're doing poems," he said.

"About grannies and grandpas," added another child.

"Before playtime the children wrote down everything they could think of about their own grandparents. So if you would like to take a seat, Mr Steel, we will see what interesting things the children have come up with. Let's start with grannies."

The children were keen to volunteer their ideas and little hands waved in the air. Their responses came so fast the

Our grandchildren accept us for ourselves,

teacher, who was writing down their thoughts, had quite a job to keep up. Soon the whiteboard at the front of the classroom was full of their thoughts:

Grannies don't walk fast, they go slowly.
They never tell you off.
They talk all the time.
They smell of flowers.
They tell you stories and sing songs.
Grannies have white hair and wrinkly faces.
They have knobbly hands.
They have lumpy cardigans and yellow beads.
They wear brown stockings.
Grannies are fat and wear glasses.
They sit in armchairs and fall asleep.
They love children but they don't have any of their own.
They can take their teeth out.
They have bad legs.
Grannies are good for cuddles.

---

without rebuke or effort to change us.

"My goodness, what a lot of ideas," said Miss Wilson. She then caught sight of a small boy who had remained silent and sombre. "What about you, Joshua?" she said. "Can you tell us something about your grannie?"

"I haven't got a grannie, Miss," said the child sadly. Bright spots of tears appeared in the corners of his eyes and he sniffed noisily.

"Of course you have," replied the teacher.

"I haven't, Miss. I've only got a nannie."

"But she's a grannie," Miss Wilson told him. The boy stopped sniffing to listen. "There are a lot of different names for grannies. You call your grannie, nannie, I used to call mine nana."

"And I used to call my grannie Flopsy Wopsy," said Mr Steel.

"I think I am going to be sick again," said Blossom.

A grandchild's laughter is the greatest medicine.